WHY SHOULD I LISTEN?

Books in the
WHY SHOULD I? Series:

WHY SHOULD I Protect Nature?   WHY SHOULD I Eat Well?
WHY SHOULD I Recycle?   WHY SHOULD I Help?
WHY SHOULD I Save Water?   WHY SHOULD I Listen?
WHY SHOULD I Save Energy?   WHY SHOULD I Share?

First edition for the United States, its territories and dependencies, and Canada published in 2005 by Barron's Educational Series, Inc.

First published in Great Britain in 2001 by Hodder Wayland, an imprint of Hodder Children's Books.
© Copyright 2001 Hodder Wayland
Hodder Children's Books
A division of Hodder Headline Ltd.
338 Euston Road
London NW1 3BH
United Kingdom
Reprinted 2002 and 2004

All inquiries should be addressed to:
Barron's Educational Series, Inc.
250 Wireless Boulevard
Hauppauge, NY 11788
www.barronseduc.com

International Standard Book Number 0-7641-3219-9

Library of Congress Catalog Card Number 2004113858

Printed in China
9 8 7 6 5 4 3 2 1

WHY SHOULD I LISTEN?

Written by Claire Llewellyn

Illustrated by Mike Gordon

BARRON'S

I can hear wonderful things
when I really listen
... a beautiful songbird

... a grasshopper on the lawn

... or the crunch of freshly fallen snow.

5

But sometimes I find it hard to listen. It's often when I'm really busy – watching TV ...

6

7

Are you joining us for gym, Joe?

or flying a rocket to the moon.

Some people ask, why should I listen?
Well … NOT listening can get you
into trouble.

11

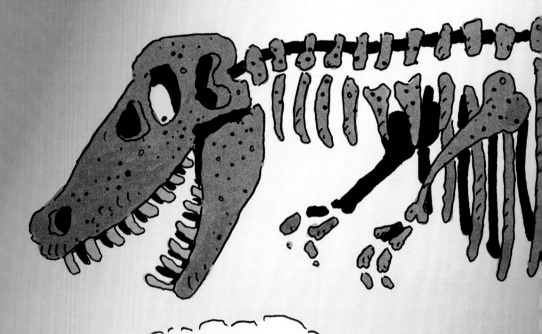

12

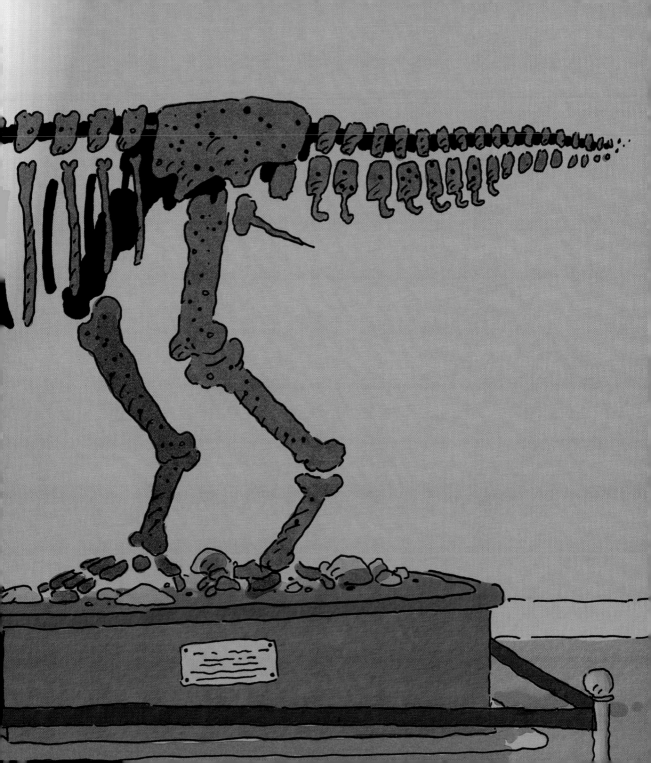

And what do you think happened at Isabel's party because I didn't hear a word she said?

Cool!

16

And guess what happened to my sister last summer when I didn't listen to my Mom?

19

20

21

23

So now when someone is talking,
I try very hard to listen.

27

And pick up the things that I need to hear.

Watch the wet paint, Joe!

You need your gym shoes tomorrow.

Notes for parents and teachers

Why Should I?

These books will help young readers to recognize what they like and dislike, what is fair and unfair, and what is right and wrong; to think about themselves, learn from their experiences, and recognize what they are good at. Some titles in this series will help to teach children how to make simple choices that improve their health and well-being, to maintain personal hygiene, and to learn rules for, and ways of, keeping safe, including basic road safety. Reading these books will help children recognize how their behavior affects other people, to listen to other people, and to play and work cooperatively, and that family and friends should care for one another.

About *Why Should I Listen?*

Why Should I Listen? is intended to be an enjoyable book that discusses the importance of listening. A variety of situations throughout this book explore the ways in which this vital skill can help children.

Listening helps children to play an active role in their families, their classes, and school. Answering a ringing phone, helping out at home, and bringing things into class are all valuable tasks for young children, helping them to feel good about themselves and preparing them for greater independence and responsibility.

Listening is vital in developing relationships with others. Listening to others helps children to work together, to learn how their behavior affects others, and to share each other's feelings. Some children find it hard to think about anything outside themselves. Learning to consider others is part of growing up.

Being listened to helps children's self-esteem and enables them to be open and express their feelings. It helps them to develop an understanding and knowledge of themselves as individuals.

Listening is important in keeping safe. Listening to the people who care for them helps children learn the basic rules and skills for keeping themselves safe. Listening for vital information, such as where it is safe to cross the road, is an important step in taking some responsibility for themselves.

Suggestions as you read the book with children

The book is full of examples of times when a child has either succeeded or failed to listen. As you come across each example, it might be useful to stop and discuss it with children. When do they find it hard to listen? Why is that?

All of us sometimes fail to listen. How would they feel if they turned up at a swimming party without their bathing suits? Has something similar ever happened to them? Talking and thinking about past disasters may help to avoid a repetition.

Being listened to is important for everyone – adults and children alike. Can they remember a time when they weren't listened to? Adults are often guilty of not listening to children. Why do they think this is? What could they say to an adult who wasn't listening to them?

Suggested follow-up activities

You could ask children to volunteer examples of their favorite sounds (the first robin, the ice cream man, or the theme song of their favorite TV program) and to draw pictures of them. Make a wall display under the heading "Listen!"

Children could write accounts of, or make up stories about, not listening. These could be put together to make a class book.

Take children for a walk. Before you go, ask them to predict what sounds they might hear on the walk (e.g., birdsong, an airplane, a dog barking, etc.). Draw symbols for about ten different sounds on a piece of paper, photocopy it, and give a copy to each child. While they are on the walk, ask them to check the symbols of any of the sounds they hear (and write down any others).

Play "Simon Says." In this game, one person is "Simon" and tells the others what to do: "Simon says, scratch your nose/touch your ear/hop on one leg," etc. Occasionally, Simon tricks the group by omitting to say the words "Simon says" before the instruction. Anyone who follows the instruction without these words is out of the game.

Books to read

Even That Moose Won't Listen to Me by Martha Alexander (Dial Books, 1988)

Listen to Me by Barbara J. Neasi and Amy Wummer (Turtleback Books, 2001)